J. Edward Evans

 Lerner Publications Company ▪ Minneapolis

This book is available in two editions:
Library binding by Lerner Publications Company
Soft cover by First Avenue Editions
241 First Avenue North
Minneapolis, MN 55401

LIBRARY OF CONGRESS CATALOGING-IN-PUBLICATION DATA

Evans, J. Edward.
  Jerry Rice: touchdown talent / J. Edward Evans.
    p. cm. – (The Achievers)
  Summary: Profiles the record-breaking receiver, from his
childhood in Mississippi to his success with the San Francisco 49ers.
  ISBN 0-8225-0521-5
  1. Rice, Jerry – Juvenile literature. 2. Football players – United
States – Biography – Juvenile literature. 3. San Francisco (49ers) –
Juvenile literature. [1. Rice, Jerry. 2. Football players. 3. Afro-
Americans – Biography.] I. Title. II. Series
GV939.R53E93   1993
796.332'092 – dc20
[B]   93-10010
                                                           CIP
                                                            AC

Manufactured in the United States of America

International Standard Book Number: 0-8225-0521-5 (lib. bdg.)
International Standard Book Number: 0-8225-9634-2 (pbk.)
Library of Congress Catalog Card Number: 93-10010

1 2 3 4 5 6 – P/JR – 98 97 96 95 94 93

3 9082 04879895 6

Contents

1 Crossing the Goal Line 7

2 Brick Road to Success 15

3 Striking Gold in
San Francisco 25

4 To the Super Bowl 39

5 Looking Good 51

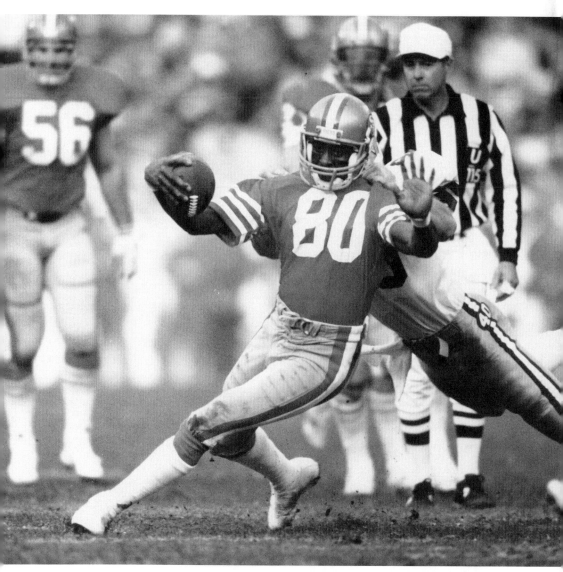

Despite his spectacular talent, Rice struggled at times during his
rookie season with the 49ers.

1
Crossing the Goal Line

The San Francisco 49ers had given their rookie wide receiver a simple task against the Kansas City Chiefs: Keep going deep. Jerry Rice was fast and had the hands. The long pass patterns would be his.

Late in the first half of this 1985 game, Rice dashed downfield. A quick fake left one defender behind, and then—with long, smooth strides—Rice broke into the clear. Quarterback Joe Montana spotted him and launched a perfect pass. As the wide receiver opened his hands to gather in the ball, no one stood between him and a 70-yard touchdown.

But as the ball floated down to him, Rice lost his concentration. His fingers seemed to turn to stone, and he dropped the football. Incomplete. No touchdown.

A groan went up from the hometown fans at San Francisco's Candlestick Park. The rookie had messed up again—his 11th muffed pass in his first 11 games as a pro. So this was the small-college wonder on whom the 49ers had wasted their top draft choice. Boos rose from the crowd and showered down on Rice. Already upset about dropping the pass, Rice was stunned by the crowd's reaction. "I hadn't been booed in all my life," he said later.

Although some fans may have been ready to give up on Jerry Rice, anyone who had watched him in practice knew better. The dropped passes were a problem, but Rice had the talent to be a star. His pass-catching teammate, Dwight Clark, knew what to expect from Rice. "The first time I saw him," said Clark, "he was the best I ever saw."

Through most of his first season in the National Football League (NFL), Rice struggled to harness that talent and hit his stride. Rice's talk about his rookie-season troubles makes that year sound like a complete bust. The numbers, however, tell a different story—49 receptions for 927 yards. That was a good set of stats, something that many veteran NFL receivers would have been proud to claim. But it was not enough to satisfy Jerry Rice. He knew that if he could settle down and quit dropping passes, he could really be somebody in the NFL. He also knew that he didn't ever want to be booed again.

Ever since he lost his rookie jitters, Rice has heard nothing but cheers from the 49er fans. In his second year as a pro, he led the league in pass-reception yardage (1,570) and in touchdown catches (15). By his third year, he was already shattering league records.

Rice has left his mark in end zones throughout the league—and in the record books. No one has caught more NFL touchdown passes than Rice (103 at the end of the 1992 season). The previous record holder, Seattle's Steve Largent, had collected 100 touchdown catches over a 14-year career. Rice's 103 scoring grabs came in only 8 seasons.

Rice strides off the field after setting a new NFL record for career touchdown receptions.

The secret to Jerry Rice's success? Perhaps it's his powerful hands.

Just what makes Jerry Rice the best at snaring touchdown passes? Some say it's his powerful hands. The first thing his college coach, Archie "Gunslinger" Cooley, noticed about Rice was that "he had those hands." Cooley's assistant coach, Gloster Richardson, saw the same thing. "He doesn't need to use his body to catch the ball," said Richardson, who had once played wide receiver in the NFL. "His hands were just a gift."

Others credit Rice's speed—even though he runs the 40-yard dash slower than the average NFL wide receiver. One man who has tried to cover him, cornerback Vestee Jackson of the Chicago Bears, thinks that Rice's 40-yard times of about 4.6 seconds are misleading. "He has a special explosion that the 4.4 guys don't have," Jackson says. Somehow, once the ball is in the air, Rice's long strides and instant acceleration can leave much faster defenders in the dust.

At least one teammate thinks Rice works his magic by faking out defenders. San Francisco quarterback Steve Young believes that "what makes him so special is his body language. I've never seen anything like it." Rice takes pride in getting defenders to think he's going one way when he plans to go another. He describes his strategy in just three words: "Bite. Shake. Gone." He has a special knack for getting an opponent to "bite"—to respond to a fake—shaking loose from the man, and then blowing past for the score.

Other observers marvel at the way Rice creates his own scoring opportunities, even in plays designed to get the ball to some other receiver. A 1991 touchdown against San Diego is a classic example of his creativity. Rice started off by running his assigned pass route to the middle of the field, but then he spotted an opening in the pass coverage. He broke off his pattern, cut quickly, and waved to let quarterback Steve Young know he wanted the ball. Young got the message and threw a 70-yard touchdown pass to his favorite receiver.

Rice and his teammates perform a familiar end zone ritual—the touchdown celebration—after another Rice score.

Maybe sheer determination has put Rice ahead of the crowd. Jerry's father once saw his young son dive into a thornbush to catch a pass thrown by an older brother. "He got stuck bad," Joe Rice remembers, "but he caught it." A former coach for San Francisco, Dennis Green, says that "when the ball is in the air, Jerry thinks it's his."

Most likely, some combination of all these traits makes Rice stand out. Whatever the reason for his success, Rice presents a special challenge to any opponent. A former head coach of the 49ers, Bill Walsh, knows football talent. He has coached many legendary players, including Joe Montana, perhaps the greatest quarterback ever to play pro football. Yet it was Jerry Rice whom Walsh called "the most dominating player in the game today."

Jerry Rice grew up in this house, which now belongs to another family. Jerry's grandfather, John T. Rice (pictured), still lives down the road from the house.

2
Brick Road to Success

As a boy, Jerry Rice did more hard physical work than most kids. Working summers for his father, a bricklayer, wasn't always fun, but it toughened him up. As it turned out, every brick he caught was a stepping stone to the top.

Jerry Lee Rice was born on October 13, 1962, in Starkville, Mississippi, to Joe and Eddie B. Rice. He was one of five boys, the fifth of eight children. He grew up near Crawford, a town of about 500 people in eastern Mississippi. His mom, Eddie B., remembers him as a quiet, skinny youngster, but a diligent one. He has, she says, "worked hard at everything he's done all his days."

Tough manual labor was a part of life for the Rice boys. Their father expected his sons to help him do brickwork when school was out for the summer. Jerry took his turn pushing the heavy wheelbarrow, stacking bricks, and shoveling mortar. The rough, sharp-edged bricks cut into his hands and scraped his knuckles. The exercise of hauling bricks helped him develop powerful arms. Long days working in the stifling July heat built up his stamina. "I got used to hard work early," Jerry remembers. "It made my hands rough, but it made me strong."

According to Joe Rice, Jerry "handled bricks better than any worker I had." In fact, the Rice boys began to make a game of Jerry's skill at catching bricks. Jerry remembers standing on a high scaffold, waiting for his brothers to throw bricks up to him from the ground. One brother would make a stack of four bricks and fling the stack up at Jerry. Sometimes the bricks would stay close together, but often they would fly every which way. Jerry's job was to catch all four of them before they landed on the scaffold or fell to the ground. He seldom missed a brick.

The Rice boys did not spend all their time at work. Even though Jerry did not participate much in organized sports during his early years, he loved to play football in the yard with his brothers. If they were looking for a different type of action, Jerry and his brothers headed for the family's seven-acre field, hoping to ride the neighbor's horses that pastured there. But the horses had to be caught first. Jerry built up his running speed by chasing down horses so that he could ride bareback.

Jerry knew that he did not want to be a bricklayer all his life. He began thinking about life beyond his small town. Crawford had many advantages for a young boy growing up. Far from big cities, it had few drug or crime problems. Yet, according to Rice, "When you live in Crawford, all you want to do is get out."

Ever since Jerry was small, he had been good at working with his hands. He had fixed his own toys and had even repaired appliances for his parents. Jerry expected to use his hands to fashion a career. He dreamed of opening his own repair shop someday.

Jerry was not an enthusiastic student. As a sophomore at B. L. Moor High School in Crawford, he decided to cut class one day. He was sneaking down the hall when an assistant principal came up behind him. When the assistant principal called his name, Jerry panicked and dashed down the hall. Later, another school official found a clever way of confronting Jerry about this hallway sprint: He wanted to know why a boy who could run so fast was not playing on the football team.

Rice agreed, half-heartedly at first, to go out for football. His mother did not like the idea of her boy knocking heads on the football field. But Jerry began to enjoy the game, and he was determined to stay with it. His interest in sports grew, and eventually he was also playing forward on the basketball team and high jumping on the track team.

His parents could not pick him up after all these practices, and no school buses ran late enough to take him home. Jerry finished each workout by running five miles back home. Those long runs over dirt roads and across fields built up his legs and made him an even better runner.

During his senior year of high school, Rice learned how to run circles around pass defenders. He caught 80 passes that year for B. L. Moor and scored 35 touchdowns. He hoped these statistics would attract the interest of Mississippi State University, just 20 miles away in Starkville. Rice knew MSU was big enough to play football against tough competition.

Even though he was the best football player to graduate from B. L. Moor High School, Jerry drew little notice from college recruiters.

B. L. Moor High School retired Rice's football number and put his jersey on display in a trophy case.

Unfortunately, few college scouts seriously considered athletes from small schools like B. L. Moor. Despite his proven ability to score touchdowns, Jerry did not attract much attention. High schools were full of kids like him: 6-foot-1, 180 pounds, able to run the 40-yard dash in about 4.8 seconds. Although Rice received a few long-distance scholarship offers, only one college actually sent an assistant coach to visit him—tiny Mississippi Valley State University. With only about 3,500 students, Mississippi Valley State was located in Itta Bena, a town of fewer than 3,000 residents in northwestern Mississippi. The Delta Devils, as the school's athletic teams were called, did not even play major-college football. Instead they played with smaller schools in a division called I-AA.

Jerry's brother Tom, who played center for Jackson State University, thought Jerry would shine in the pass-oriented offense at Mississippi Valley State.

Although Mississippi Valley State did not seem to have much to offer, Jerry's older brother Tom advised him to consider going there. Tom Rice had played college football at Jackson State, which was in the same conference as Mississippi Valley. He knew why Mississippi Valley's head coach, Archie Cooley, was called "Gunslinger": Cooley ran a high-powered passing attack. Tom Rice thought it was just the kind of game plan that would let a wide receiver shine.

Jerry signed on with the Delta Devils in 1981. While working on his football skills in Itta Bena, he concentrated on classes in technical subjects. He still thought that his most likely career would be as an auto mechanic or an electrician.

Rice felt comfortable right away with Coach Cooley's "Satellite Express" passing attack. In his first college season, Jerry caught 30 passes, and he more than doubled that (to 66 receptions) as a sophomore. In one game against Tennessee State, Rice gained 279 yards on pass receptions.

Coach Cooley marveled at Rice's ability, remarking that he could "catch a BB in the dark." In 1983 Cooley and his assistant, Gloster Richardson, designed their offense to get the ball to Rice whenever possible. On October 1, 1983, Rice put in the busiest day of any receiver in the history of Division I-AA college football. He made 24 receptions, not counting 4 other catches that were erased by penalties. By the end of his junior year, Rice had broken the Division I-AA career record for pass receptions, and he still had another year of college ball to play. Teammates and fans started calling him "World," because it seemed there was nothing in the world he could not catch.

Rather than growing smug about his success, Rice kept working harder. During his senior year, he and quarterback Willie Totten arrived early for most practices so they could get a few extra minutes to refine their timing.

Rice was nearly unstoppable during his senior year. Opposing coaches regularly assigned two players to guard him, but they still couldn't keep him out of the end zone. Before finishing his career at Mississippi

Valley State, Rice set a total of 18 Division I-AA records, including an incredible 27 touchdowns during his senior year. He caught more than 100 passes in each of his final two years. During his college football career, he gained 4,693 yards on receptions and scored 50 touchdowns.

Those numbers brought pro scouts streaming down to Itta Bena to take a look. They loved Rice's confident, aggressive attitude. He would run any type of pass pattern without fear of being hit. Rice also knew what to do with the ball after he caught it. "I'm always looking to turn it upfield and run over some people," he said. Having grown to 6 feet, 3 inches, and having beefed up to 205 pounds, Rice was big enough to do just that.

Rice (left) and quarterback Willie Totten were the number one passing-receiving combination in NCAA Division I-AA during 1984. Many of the records they set that year have never been broken.

The big question pro scouts had about Jerry: Would he still be a star playing against tougher defenders in the National Football League?

But when the scouts started studying him carefully, they found faults. Although Rice was advertised as a speed runner, his times in the 40-yard dash were nothing special. Rice's only job at Mississippi Valley State had been to catch the ball; he knew little about blocking. Scouts kept saying that he had not played against top-level competition in college. Many doubted that he could handle the big jump from Division I-AA ball to the pros.

Still, a few NFL teams had no doubts about Jerry Rice. One of these teams was the Dallas Cowboys. Jerry Rice would probably have performed his NFL magic for the Cowboys if it were not for a sleepless night suffered by San Francisco head coach Bill Walsh.

3

Striking Gold in San Francisco

In October 1984, the San Francisco 49ers traveled to Houston for a game against the Oilers. The night before the game, Coach Bill Walsh could not push the Oilers out of his mind. Eventually, he gave up trying to sleep and flicked on the television in his hotel room.

When the sports report came on, Walsh watched a highlight clip that showed a tall, graceful football player in a green-and-red uniform catching a touchdown pass. This same player, number 88, caught another touchdown pass. Then another. And another. By the time Walsh had watched the fifth touchdown reception by this star from Mississippi Valley State, he was wide awake. He knew he had seen something special. "As soon as I saw him run and catch," said Walsh, "I knew that if we didn't get him, someday we'd be playing against him."

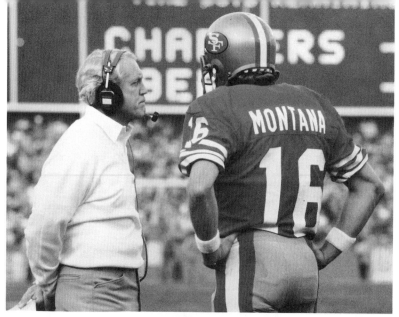

When San Francisco coach Bill Walsh saw Rice on news highlight films, the 49ers were on their way to a second Super Bowl victory.

After asking the 49ers' scouts to take a special look at the Itta Bena star, Walsh contacted Rice's coach. Coach Cooley sent Walsh reels of film showing his star wide receiver in action. Not everyone in the 49er organization saw as much star quality as Walsh saw. One scout pegged Rice as maybe a fifth- or sixth-round choice in the NFL's annual draft of college players.

Walsh, however, was certain that Rice would be taken in the first round. In the NFL, teams draft in order of their previous-season records, with the worst teams choosing first. The 49ers, the Super Bowl champions, would be last in line. The Dallas Cowboys would be drafting well ahead of them, and the Cowboys were in desperate need of a wide receiver.

After Al Toon of the University of Wisconsin and Eddie Brown of Miami University were selected early in the first round, only Rice remained a likely choice for the Cowboys.

The draft moved through the first round until the only team still to pick before the Cowboys was New England. Dallas knew that the New England Patriots were not interested in Rice, so nothing seemed to stand between Rice and a Cowboy uniform. But Walsh wanted Rice so much that he made New England a last-minute offer they could not refuse. If the Patriots would let the 49ers take New England's spot in the first-round drafting order, the 49ers would give New England three draft spots—their first-, second-, and third-round picks. With that move, San Francisco snatched Rice away from the Cowboys.

A number of San Francisco sportswriters had heard that some 49er scouts had doubts about Rice. Some writers were especially upset that the 49ers had given so much to New England to get this untested small-college receiver.

Their first look at the timid rookie only convinced the skeptical reporters that this new guy was from the backwoods. Rice had played his entire college career far from the big cities. He had rarely seen more than a couple of reporters in one place. In his first few days in San Francisco, reporters seemed to be swarming all over the place. "I was so shy when I first came here

I was afraid to say anything," Rice said. "I was scared to death."

There were other changes. At Mississippi Valley State, Rice had been "World"—by far the biggest star in the school's history. Suddenly, he was just some college guy trying to prove he belonged on the same field with the Super Bowl champions. He could not even wear his college number, "88," because one of the veterans already had it.

Rice had to learn an entirely new way of playing his position. With the Delta Devils, Rice had been the main threat on nearly every play. Although he ran assigned pass patterns as well as anyone, he also had the freedom in college play to break out of a pattern if he thought another route would work better. San Francisco's complicated offense did not allow him that kind of creativity. Rice had a job to do on each play—a particular pattern to run—and he was expected to do it. If he fell back into his old habits and changed his route during a practice session, he'd get a chewing out from an angry coach.

Rice, who had so confidently knocked over defensive backs in college, found that the pros were not scared of him. Some defensive backs liked to meet him right at the line of scrimmage and knock him off his pass route. Some of the more aggressive defenders tried to knock him off his feet. For a while, football stopped being fun. Rice grew frustrated with it all—

his reduced status, the bump-and-run defenders, the mental strain of remembering every play in the 49ers' thick playbook. When he did get open for a pass, he was often so out of rhythm that he dropped the ball.

After that happened a few times, he tried too hard to make up for his mistakes. Quarterback Joe Montana remembers Rice trying to turn every catch into a touchdown. Because of this obsession with the goal line, Jerry sometimes started running with the ball before he had a firm hold on it. Many easy catches fell out of his grasp. For a while, he tried wearing gloves on the field, in hopes that they might help him hang on to the ball. It didn't work.

During his rookie season, Jerry tried too hard to score every time he had the ball.

Looking back on those early days, Rice thinks that his problems on the field resulted from huge changes in his life-style. He was in the big city for the first time in his life, with far more money than he had ever had. Between practices, he spent much of his time cruising the town and buying whatever he wanted. With these distractions, he lost his concentration and started dropping passes. Then the problem fed on itself: Once he had dropped a few balls, he lost his confidence and dropped even more.

Veteran receivers Dwight Clark and Freddie Solomon, however, helped their new teammate settle into his position.

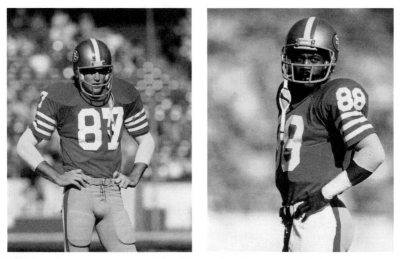

Veteran receivers Dwight Clark (left) and Freddie Solomon (right) helped Rice learn how to use his talents better against NFL defenders.

They taught him some tricks for beating bump-and-run coverage. They helped him recognize different types of zone pass coverage. Even after Rice beat Solomon out for a spot in the starting lineup, the unselfish veteran continued to encourage the rookie and show him ways to improve his game.

Rice learned his lessons well, but that first season was hardly "The Jerry Rice Show." Not until the 14th game of the 1985 season did Rice flash some of his college brilliance. Playing in a nationally televised game against the Los Angeles Rams, he caught 10 passes for 241 yards and a touchdown. That late-season burst helped him win the National Football Conference's rookie-of-the-year honors. The season ended on a sour note, however. The 49ers were shut down by the New York Giants in the first round of post-season action. Rice caught only 4 passes for 45 yards, as his team failed to score a touchdown in a 17-3 loss.

By the start of the 1986 season, his second in the NFL, Rice had adjusted to the challenges of playing with the pros. He had learned to relax and to trust his own abilities both on and off the field. The shy kid who could hardly talk to the press had become a confident professional, comfortable enough in the spotlight to consider a post-football career in radio and television. He even began taking speech lessons with that in mind.

Rice was eager to put the bobbles of his rookie season behind him. An early-season contest against the Indianapolis Colts in 1986 gave him a chance to do just that. Rice caught 6 passes for 172 yards, including touchdown receptions of 58, 45, and 16 yards. "There was something about that game that put me on track," Rice said.

Rice was so firmly on track that in 1986 he led the entire league both in pass-reception yardage (1,570) and in touchdown catches (15). Only two players in the history of the NFL (Charley Hennigan and Lance Alworth) had gained more yards on receptions in a season than Rice. On two occasions that year, Rice scored three touchdowns in a game. *Sports Illustrated* magazine thought so highly of his performance that they named him the Player of the Year in the National Football Conference (NFC).

After that successful 1986 regular season, however—just when he was riding high—his brick-battered hands failed him again. The 49ers, in the play-offs again, were eager to avenge their loss to the Giants early in the 1985 play-offs. But they drew a tough assignment. They had to travel to New York to battle the hard-hitting Giants on their home field.

In the first quarter of that contest, Rice glided behind the Giants' defense and gathered in a pass from Joe Montana. Rice tucked the ball away and started to run. He had clear sailing to the end zone, but just as 49er fans were chalking up six points for their team, Rice dropped the ball. No one even touched him. The ball simply fell out of his hands.

Jerry runs with the ball in the play-off game against the New York Giants. His first-quarter fumble was a sign of things to come for the 49ers during the rest of the game.

The Giants took advantage of the gift and jumped to an early lead. They went on to pound the 49ers by a score of 49-3. "That play will always linger in the back of my mind," said Rice. Without taking a single day off to rest after that play-off loss, Rice started in on tough workouts to prepare for the next season.

Rice's 1987 season was shortened because he and many other NFL players went on strike for part of the season. Playing in only 12 games that year, he did not catch the ball as often nor gain nearly as many yards—"only" 65 passes for 1,078 yards—as he had the year before. But Jerry Rice did drop a few strong hints in 1987 that he could become the highest-scoring pass receiver ever to play NFL football. Opposing teams could not keep him out of the end zone.

Rice started things rolling in the season's second game by rescuing the 49ers from certain defeat. San Francisco was losing to the Cincinnati Bengals, and the game clock showed only enough time for one more play. All the Cincinnati defensive backs hung back and paid special attention to Jerry, but he found a way to slip free. As time ran out, he caught a pass in the end zone to win the game.

Adding to a streak that he started in 1986, Rice managed in 1987 to log his 13th straight game with at least one touchdown catch. That set a new NFL record, eclipsing the old mark of 11 straight (shared by Elroy Hirsch and Buddy Dial). But Rice's most impressive feat of 1987 was his NFL record for touchdown catches in a season. Until Jerry went wild that year, Miami's Mark Clayton had held the record—thanks to the 18 scoring catches he made during 16 games in 1984. In 1987 Rice brought 22 passes into the end zone in just 12 games!

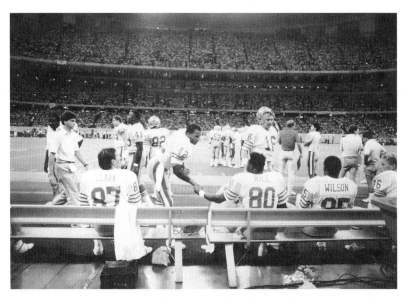

After another successful drive, the offensive unit takes a break on the sidelines.

After racking up a 14-2 record during the regular season, the 49ers were strong favorites to advance to the Super Bowl. In the first round of play-off action, however, they were ambushed by the underdog Minnesota Vikings. The 36-24 defeat stung all the more for Rice because he had been completely upstaged by Minnesota's star wide receiver, Anthony Carter. Hobbled by a sore leg, Rice contributed little to the 49ers' effort—only 3 receptions for 28 yards and no touchdowns. Carter, however, caught 10 passes, many of them spectacular acrobatic grabs, for a play-off record of 227 yards.

That game was a shock to Jerry Rice. Just a few weeks earlier, he had been praised as the best wide receiver ever to play the game. Now Rice was ignored while Carter grabbed the headlines and the praise. Some football critics whispered that Jerry Rice might not have what it takes to be a champion, that he couldn't stand up to the pressure of the big games. In three years of play-off action, Rice had not caught a single touchdown pass. Looking back on his record-breaking 1987 season, Rice said that he was proud of what he'd done, but because his team had been eliminated early in the play-offs, it didn't mean a thing.

The Rices, Jerry, Jacqui (center), and Jackie (right) ride in the Super Bowl parade.

4
To the Super Bowl

The 1988 season only added to Rice's frustration. He injured his ankle early, and it never completely healed that year. Unable to come through with his usual sharp cuts and bursts of speed, Rice suffered through his most disappointing season. The 49ers struggled along with him for most of the year. The team seemed unlikely even to make the play-offs that year. Only a late-season winning streak allowed them to squeak past the New Orleans Saints and the Los Angeles Rams in the race for the NFC's Western Division title.

Rice had a lot to prove as the first play-off game drew near. Although his season total of 64 catches for 1,306 yards was excellent by most standards, it did not match his expectations. Worst of all, Rice's total of touchdown receptions had plunged to nine. Once again, the 49ers would begin the play-offs by hosting the powerful Minnesota Vikings and their ace receiver,

Anthony Carter. Rice did not want to see Carter out-play him again.

Rice performed no spectacular tricks against the Vikings. Instead he was quietly, ruthlessly efficient. In the first quarter he helped his team to an early lead by catching a 2-yard touchdown pass. Later in the first half, he spun away from a defender to score on a 4-yard pass. As Rice pranced into the end zone on an 11-yard score just before halftime, the 49ers were clearly in command. This time Carter stood in the shadows as Rice and the 49ers rolled to a 34-9 win.

Rice, getting a block from quarterback Joe Montana on this play, had three touchdowns in the first half to lead San Francisco over Minnesota.

Another touchdown for Jerry! This one came against the Bears in the frigid climate of Soldier Field in Chicago.

The 49ers moved on to the NFC championship game. Many football fans expected the 49ers' offense to stall against the tough Chicago Bears—and the cold weather—at Chicago's Soldier Field. But with his streak of scoreless play-offs finally broken and his ankle feeling better than it had all year, Rice felt confident. "I'll catch the ball in any kind of weather," he told reporters. In fact, Rice predicted that he would have a great game. "I'm healthy now," he said, "and that makes all the difference."

A fierce wind blasted Rice as he trotted onto the field to warm up. The temperature was 17°F. It was the coldest weather the Mississippi native had ever played in. In the first quarter, San Francisco's offense was sputtering. It seemed that Bear weather had struck after all. Then, on a difficult third-and-10 play at Chicago's 39-yard line, Joe Montana stepped back to pass. Facing an awesome blitz by the Bears, he rushed a pass toward the right sideline. Jerry Rice leaped high, stuck up his hands, and snatched the hard, frozen football out of the air. He faked one Bear defensive back off balance, then cut past another. In a flash, Rice was sprinting all alone down the frozen field. His 61-yard touchdown play and Mike Cofer's extra point put San Francisco on top, 7-0.

In the second quarter, the blitzing Bears again swarmed in on Montana as he tried a pass. The play was designed to go to another receiver, but Montana caught sight of Rice, who was breaking over the middle. Montana tossed a low pass that reached Rice about 12 yards from the line of scrimmage. Rice had to reach down to his shoe tops for the ball, but he snared it, tucked it under his arm, and dashed the final 15 yards for another score.

Chicago never recovered from Rice's quick strikes. San Francisco coasted to a 28-3 win and the right to play Super Bowl XXIII against the Cincinnati Bengals in Miami.

San Francisco's reward for winning in Chicago was a trip to Miami for Super Bowl XXIII at Joe Robbie Stadium.

With five catches for 133 yards against the Bears, Rice had destroyed any doubts about his big-game ability. Even more important, he had made five touchdown receptions in his last two play-off games. The Super Bowl, however, turned the pressure up yet another notch. How would Rice respond to the most important game of all?

The pre-Super Bowl week started out bad. During a workout on the Monday before the game, Rice twisted the same ankle that had bothered him for most of the year. Many Bengals thought that Rice was faking it, exaggerating the injury just to make them think he would not be at full speed. But Rice and the 49ers were not certain if he would be able to play at all. "I won't know whether I can cut on it until game time," Rice said.

The NFL puts on quite a show for the Super Bowl.

Rice was in uniform on January 22, 1989, as the 49ers took the field against the Bengals. The loose sod in Miami's Joe Robbie Stadium made cutting (suddenly changing directions) treacherous, even for those with healthy legs and ankles. Early in the first quarter, the Bengals' ace defensive lineman, Tim Krumrie, broke his left leg in two places when he planted his foot. The loose turf would be especially punishing to a tender ankle, but Rice decided to play anyway.

San Francisco counted on its offense to have a productive day both running and passing. But, despite a fine performance by Rice, the 49er offense produced nothing but one field goal in the first half. Fortunately for the Niners, the Bengal offense was equally sluggish. The teams left the field at halftime tied at 3-3.

Things seemed only to get worse for San Francisco in the second half, especially when Cincinnati's Stanford Jennings fielded a San Francisco kick and took off. Jennings sprinted straight through the 49ers' kick-coverage squad and into the end zone—a 93-yard touchdown that gave Cincinnati a 13-6 lead in the third quarter.

This jolted the 49ers into action. Showing signs of their usual precision, San Francisco drove downfield to the Bengal 14-yard line early in the fourth quarter. Would San Francisco waste yet another scoring chance? Not if Jerry Rice could help it. His ankle was beginning to throb from the stress of sharp moves on loose turf, but Rice planted his foot one more time and broke toward the sideline to snare a pass from Montana. Most receivers would have been content to make the catch and hold on to the ball while being knocked out of bounds.

Jerry Rice was not most receivers. He did a tightrope dance along the sidelines. As he was tackled, he lunged and squirmed and stretched toward the end zone. Somehow he nudged the ball across the goal line before he hit the ground. That touchdown, and the extra point that came after it, tied the game at 13-13.

Cincinnati, however, was not dead yet. An impressive drive brought them into field-goal range with less than four minutes remaining in the game. Jim Breech booted his third field goal of the game to put the Bengals back on top, 16-13.

Backed up to their own 10-yard line and with just over three minutes to play, the 49ers knew they would have no more second chances. If they did not score on this drive, the Super Bowl was lost.

Jerry Rice hobbled onto the field to begin the final drive. Had it been a regular game, Rice probably would have stayed on the sidelines to nurse his injured ankle. But this was the Super Bowl, and Rice was determined to give everything he had left to give. As Coach Bill Walsh later said about that last drive, "Jerry Rice was operating on nerve." Rice remembers the grim silence of his teammates as they set out to beat both the Bengals and the clock. "When Joe [Montana] came into the huddle, you could have heard a pin drop."

The 49ers kept their poise and marched steadily downfield. Eight quick plays, including two short passes to Rice, carried San Francisco to the Bengals' 35-yard line. The Niners were almost within field-goal range. "I was just thinking about getting a field goal to tie the game and send it into overtime," Montana later said. But suddenly San Francisco's precise offense began to unravel. Montana threw an incomplete pass. Then offensive lineman Randy Cross was penalized for being downfield illegally on a screen pass. That brought the ball back to the Bengals' 45-yard line.

Could San Francisco's top passing combination—Montana to Rice—come through again?

Faced with a difficult situation—second down and 20, one minute remaining—Montana had to aim for some serious yardage. The time for conservative short-gain play was over.

The next play called for Jerry Rice to run a few yards downfield and then cut in toward the middle. Because the 49ers obviously had to pass the ball, Rice would attract a lot of Bengal defenders. But the 49ers hoped that Rice could manage to latch onto the ball, even in all that traffic, and perhaps gain 10 or 12 yards. That would put San Francisco just within field-goal range and still leave time for another play that might get them even closer.

Jerry Rice, however, was not thinking about a field goal. Ignoring the pain in his ankle, he cut across the middle and looked back for the ball. Montana had to thread his pass through the arms of several Bengal defenders. Rice had to concentrate hard to catch the ball while Bengals zoomed at him from all directions. The Montana-Rice pass machine, however, was in tune and humming. Rice made the catch at the Bengals' 32-yard line and then broke away from tacklers to charge downfield for another 14 yards and a first down. This gave the 49ers a few more downs to work with—and hope for a winning touchdown instead of a tying field goal.

Two plays later it came. While Rice kept several Bengal defenders busy, another wide receiver, John

Taylor, broke free in the end zone. Montana fired a 10-yard scoring pass to Taylor to win the game.

Rice's totals for the day were 11 catches, for a Super Bowl record of 215 yards, and one touchdown. Even Montana's brilliance under pressure on the final drive could not compare with Rice's performance. Jerry easily captured the Most Valuable Player Award for Super Bowl XXIII. Cincinnati head coach Sam Wyche agreed with the choice. "Rice was the difference in the game," he said.

5
Looking Good

Scouting reports on Jerry Rice say that he catches the ball well in a crowd. That may be the only thing that he does well in a crowd. Rice likes his privacy and does not deal very well with mobs of people. Although he lives on the outskirts of San Francisco, he rarely visits the city. He dislikes the traffic.

Rice gets along well with his teammates. But even among teammates, he is careful to protect his own space. After the 49ers' winning drive in Super Bowl XXIII—one of the finest team efforts in sports history—Rice retreated, by himself, to a quiet spot in the locker room. Only after he had spent a few moments alone did he rejoin his teammates for the victory celebration.

Jerry prefers to spend most of his free time with his family, and he enjoys being an active, involved father. He and his wife, Jackie—his former college sweetheart—had their first child, a daughter named Jacqui, in 1987. When Jacqui was an infant, it was Jerry who volunteered for night duty. "I'll be lying there dead asleep and Jerry will hear the baby before I do," said Jackie. "He's the one to get up and take care of her." Jerry and Jackie also have a son, Jerry Jr., who was born in 1991.

Jerry seems as comfortable running a vacuum cleaner as running a deep pass pattern. Jackie Rice says that when her husband gets home from a game, the first thing he does is start cleaning the house.

Left: Jerry was a natural in his new role as a dad. He was the first to hear Jacqui requesting her nighttime feedings. Opposite page: The Rice family grew larger when Jerry Jr. was born in 1991. From left to right: Jerry Jr., Jerry Sr., Jacqui, and Jackie pose on a motorcycle for a family portrait.

Rice likes to keep his personal appearance as tidy as his house. Many football players cultivate a down-and-dirty, grass-stained image. But Rice likes to keep his fingernails clean. He often takes three showers a day. Off the field, he is known as one of his team's flashiest dressers. On the field, Rice is in a class by himself. He often spends as much as two hours putting on his uniform before a game—just to make sure everything is perfect. His helmet has to be spotless and his shirt tucked in neatly. He has a special way of taping his shoes and knows just how high he wants his white socks pulled up. Rice keeps a clean towel tucked in his belt so he can wipe his hands if they get dirty or wet. "For me to play good, I have to look good," he explains.

He certainly looked good during the 1989 season. Never satisfied with his performance, not even after his Super Bowl success, Rice reported to training camp 15 pounds lighter than his normal 205-pound playing weight. He hoped that, having shed that weight, he would be quicker than ever.

Rice put together another fabulous season in 1989. He caught 82 passes for 1,483 yards and 17 touchdowns. He also helped his newer teammates develop. While defenders focused their attention on Rice, fellow wide receiver John Taylor was able to show star quality, catching 60 passes for 1,077 yards and 10 touchdowns.

In 1989 the 49ers dominated their opponents, and Rice again was spectacular.

With Rice and Taylor catching passes, Joe Montana at the top of his game, and Roger Craig and Tom Rathman providing tough running yards, the 49ers steamrolled their opponents that year. They posted a 14-2 regular-season mark, the best in the NFL. That was only a warm-up for what was to come in the play-offs. In their opening play-off game, the 49ers thrashed the much-feared Minnesota Viking defense in a 41-13 romp. Then they crushed the Los Angeles Rams 30-3 in the NFC title game.

With plenty of distance between him and the defender, Jerry waits for the ball to settle in his hands. He and the 49ers embarrassed Denver in Super Bowl XXIV to win back-to-back championships.

San Francisco had so dominated the league in 1989 that most observers wrote off their Super Bowl XXIV contest against the Denver Broncos as a mismatch. Thanks to Montana and Rice, it was. San Francisco claimed the most lopsided Super Bowl victory in history, with a score of 55-10. Rice's contributions included seven catches for 148 yards and three touchdowns.

San Francisco had rolled through the play-offs and Super Bowl XXIV with incredible ease. As long as Rice, Montana, and their supporting cast were on stage, how could any other team even come close to putting on a good show? The 1990 season, however, was not to be a "threepeat" performance. Rice did his part in 1990, catching a career-record 100 passes for 1,502 yards. Thirteen of those catches went for touchdowns, a total that topped the league for the fourth time in five years. But this time, the 49ers ran into their old play-off rival, the New York Giants, in the NFC championship game. A last-second field goal nipped the 49ers and spoiled their chance to become the first team to win three straight Super Bowls.

In 1991 Rice's totals trailed off slightly to 80 catches for 1,206 yards. But he still showed that special knack for crossing the goal line. Rice scored 14 times on pass plays to lead the NFL again in that category. Unfortunately, the 49ers could not recover from a horrible start. Although they appeared to be one of the best teams in the league at the end of the season, they failed to make the play-offs for the first time in Rice's career.

Then came 1992. It was a good season for the 49ers, who were a play-off team once again. Until they lost the NFC championship to the Dallas Cowboys, the Niners seemed like good bets to win another Super Bowl.

But Jerry Rice will remember 1992 mostly for one rainy Sunday in Candlestick Park. When the 49ers took the field that day against the Miami Dolphins, all eyes were on Rice. He needed only one more touchdown catch to break Steve Largent's career record of 100 scoring receptions. The season was winding down quickly now, and the pressure was on. Rice had made a career of shattering records, but this was the big one.

The cold, steady rain made the field slippery and the ball slick. For more than three quarters, the magic catch eluded Rice. Then, with less than nine minutes remaining, he ran a slant pattern across the middle and shook off Miami's J. B. Brown. Steve Young's 12-yard pass was right on target, and Jerry Rice made the 101st touchdown catch of his career.

His teammates on the bench threw off their rain gear and ran to congratulate him. The San Francisco fans went wild. Holding the wet football high in the air, Jerry Rice savored the moment. "I've been chasing this for a long, long time," he said later. In only 8 seasons as a pro, he had broken a record that Largent had set in 14.

In those eight years, Jerry Rice showed that he is good enough, even on a bad day, to shred opposing defenses. Perhaps the game that showed Rice at his very best was a contest against the Atlanta Falcons on October 14, 1990.

Rice works hard on the field, and he eventually comes up with a
big play or two...or more.

Early in the game, Rice and Montana seemed unable to connect for the score. Twice, they failed to make anything out of great touchdown opportunities. Many receivers would have been discouraged at seeing two good scoring chances slip away. But Rice shrugged off the disappointment and went on to play his greatest game as a pro. He so thoroughly baffled the Atlanta defense that it almost looked as if Montana and Rice were simply out there playing catch. Rice tied an NFL record by catching *five* touchdown passes before calling it a day.

The Falcons had learned that you can't keep Jerry Rice down. You may shut him down once or twice, or for a quarter or two, but eventually he will get free. As the 49ers' Ronnie Lott, a future Hall of Fame defensive back said, "I've seen them all play. Jerry is the best. It's not even close."

JERRY RICE'S FOOTBALL STATISTICS

Mississippi Valley State University—regular season

YEAR	GAMES PLAYED	PASS RECEPTIONS	YARDS	AVERAGE	TOUCHDOWN RECEPTIONS
1981	11	30	428	14.3	2
1982	10	66	1,133	17.2	7
1983	10	102	1,450	14.2	14
1984	10	103	1,682	16.3	27
TOTALS	41	301	4,693	15.6	50

College Highlights:
All-America, 1983, 1984.
Blue-Gray game, Most Valuable Player, 1984.
Freedom Bowl All-Star game, 1984.

NCAA Division I-AA receiving records:
Most receptions, game (24), October 1, 1983.
Most receptions, career (301), 1981–1984.
Most yards gained, season (1,682), 1984.
Most yards gained, career (4,693), 1981–1984.
Most 100-yard games, career (23), 1981–1984.
Most touchdown receptions, game (5—tie) September 1 and October 27, 1984.
Most touchdown receptions, season (27), 1984.
Most touchdown receptions, career (50), 1981–1984.
Most games with a touchdown reception, season (10), 1984.
Most games with a touchdown reception, career (26), 1981–1984.
Most receptions per game, career (7.3), 1981–1984.
Most receiving yards gained per game, season (168.2), 1984.
Most receiving yards gained per game, career (114.5), 1981–1984.
Most touchdown receptions per game, season (2.7), 1984.
Most touchdown receptions per game, career (1.22), 1981–1984.

San Francisco 49ers – regular season

YEAR	GAMES PLAYED	PASS RECEPTIONS	YARDS	AVERAGE	TOUCHDOWN RECEPTIONS
1985	16	49	927	18.9	3
1986	16	86	1,570	18.3	15
1987*	12	65	1,078	16.6	22
1988	16	64	1,306	20.4	9
1989	16	82	1,483	18.1	17
1990	16	100	1,502	15.0	13
1991	16	80	1,206	15.1	14
1992	16	84	1,201	14.3	10
TOTALS	124	610	10,273	16.8	103

*players' strike year

Career Highlights:

All-Rookie, 1985.
NFC Rookie of the Year, 1985.
All-Pro, 1986, 1987, 1988, 1989, 1990, 1992.
Pro Bowl game, 1987, 1988, 1989, 1990, 1991, 1992, 1993.
NFL Player of the Year, 1987, 1990.
Super Bowl Most Valuable Player, 1989.

NFL Records:

Most consecutive games with a touchdown reception (13), 1986–87.
Most touchdown receptions, game (5—tie), October 14, 1990.
Most touchdown receptions, season (22), 1987.
Most touchdown receptions, career (103—through 1992 season).

63

ACKNOWLEDGMENTS

Photographs are reproduced with the permission of: John Biever, pp. 1, 12; Micky Pfleger, pp. 2, 6, 9, 10, 24, 26, 29, 30 (both), 33, 34, 36, 38, 40, 41, 47, 50, 52, 55, 59, 60, 64; Frank Roberts, pp. 14, 18 (both), 19, 53; Jackson State University, p. 20; Chuck Prophet/Mississippi Valley State University, pp. 22, 23; and Vernon Biever, pp. 43, 44, 56.

Front and back cover photographs are reproduced by permission of Micky Pfleger.